Late Morning When the World Burns

Late Morning When the World Burns

Shamala Gallagher

The Cultural Society
Brooklyn
MMXIX

Late Morning When the World Burns
978-0-9994912-4-9
© 2019 by Shamala Gallagher

For permission to reprint more than a few lines from this book
or for other inquiries, please write to The Cultural Society:
culturalsociety.org
publisher@culturalsociety.org

for my neighbors

CONTENTS

Take up the blood from the grass, sun.
Take it up.
These people do not thirst for it.

—Henry Dumas, *Kef 12*

Start by Asking Will There Be More

Braless slow evening. The brain

       a heavy fruit.
                 Eating raisins night.

We start in the green
      broken country.

           Someone's slave-pain loose
           in the soil. Some sweat
           loose in the soil.

The ice-poles loosening.

One hundred seven degrees
           in San Francisco.

       Here on the green
       straggle-yards,
       a glaze of chill
       in the heat-amber: &

Snot all world-thick
in the throat,

       eating raisins, eating
       cake, eating
       strawberries, sour
       gummies,

wrappers twined
in the grass,

Teenagers
                    with wine-bottles
                    beneath the table,

prickled-chin
                    hags beneath the table...

Ashtrays of rain:
amber syrup,

                    the world-scene
                    blinks out. Then returns.

Stunned water in the bayous,
                    ants red-hot,

listless-hag daughters,

one town in the wet green heat-
                    country where we squat

                    to watch the hills

melt. Ice loosening

at the earth's tip is green
                    heat here.
Some screen-burned face

looks up now.
                    Someday

the screens will blink off

in one hot breath. We'll lock

eyes & eat
    a last fruit.

Athens, Georgia

who that is bare &
looks again at the raininess first:
street-haunted, other tarot

night eats spite
from its own hands

hardened wraiths
of burning are sharp in the eyes

no page is
bare ever

the page of this street is
not bare

I've come to the right
place to hunt for madness

past a line of burning

mules and
men and cane

now I live
in the South: wake up

sharpened & wake
where is the canebrake

others stilted in the rattle

to speak in my own
ears. I am tired
I want to eat from the ground

Late Morning

Late morning & the world burns.   I cannot
                              believe it.
         So caught am I gazing
              at my own aging face.

Late morning, late August.

Late morning & Lexapro.   The world burns &
                              sometimes we watch.

Slivers of a burnt-world morning.
         The South is wild-green & historic

& on the street it blurs. I see into
         the face of a slave.   Then the street

is street again. Then the street

is basketball & shouts at the night.   Late morning—

The reef is dying
                  says Kristen. She's crying.
It's 18 million years old & it's dying.

Late morning. Insistence is a strange deer

one day in the yard,
              the grass longer. The hummingbird feeder

unvisited for weeks. Then Adam yells out: he's here!

He!   & so someone black-quick is tipped-beak,

genderblurred, maze-flitting, *there*

& nights: the families porch-gather

& if this is burning,
late-morning, if this is
the burnt-heart
world, and it is,

let me stand in the street at the white-hot

on the elbow's crook, on the thumb &
other. In my eyes let me slave &
not, slave & knot. Let my eyes go full. I want
a burnt heart if the world's burnt. Late morning.

Sweet oils for the wrinkles
                     on my face.

Eating raisins night.
               Midnight Adam sneaks

into the chocolates.

Basketballs and shouts: evening.
                  Teenagers near the river.

Braless slow evening. The brain a heavy
                  fruit. Failure all blue-knotted,

blue-eaten midnight berries,
         walls of the house

7

furred & dusted. Demetrius

is seven and looking to be hired
          by Adam. All the neighborhood

boys at the door. Want Adam.

Sand is in a six a.m. soliloquy: moon-stained
          skin. I can see her

through the cheap slats
          of my study. Late morning: all
times at once. Late morning.

Adam plays records.

 White voices with black
          songs in the mouths—too
sweet.

          Grown-out crabgrass. Lou

complains:
the cat has kittens. Lexapro:
                    I take a swamp-dark
brain to Lou's house.

I like your dress, she says. Wretch-me.
Sleep is a shut door.

Four tiny-mouths look
          up with eyes.

Shut door, late morning, against
          the ending-world. It is nine p.m.

One night's clamor of cat-voices.

Late morning, the night

a shut face.
The eyes are facing

forward. Sand is drunk
              and has words
in her teeth. I am always

waving at the neighbors, smiling. Friday

night: alone is an unbearable
          bauble, the South in my face.

Late morning, one gift
for the evening's end.
              Oh, pill-wonder.

Skirt fallen open, black
              hairs. The feeders

squirrel-taken. The squirrel's skull

quick in the rain.

              Late morning.
              The rain
              makes the world a room

and the men are
          drunk. Will the world
end and we will stay

                    in our houses?
Will I never stand
          on Sand's porch with

her, intertwining
          monologues as the thunder

gathers? I have given up drink

and am impatient
                    because I wanted

my soul drunk in return.

wisteria & loud feelings

dear someone who is not night, who
is peeling glitter polish from her own nails,
who is talking & talking to three a.m.
women in the months leading up
to her historic season of mania, June,
high on three a.m. confession
to women—I love women, I love
the dark tether of their hearts and the hidden
erratic singing, & some days it is spring in the haunted
terrain, it is spring of ragged blossoms
that race over leaning-in mill houses,
spring & the old plantations are well-kept
polished white, and I tuck my mother's
saris into a closet, one is red & gold
& I married in it, my hands smell
of coffee now, one sari is a stinging
deep pink like a curse from the bravest mouth

tear down the architecture, tear it /
tear it & down with the stubborn columns

burr & red spine of the flower: burr
& grate: teeth of the lizard: flower

teeth: I live in the south which is
not mine to tear down: I live in a half-

white body whose long arms are mine

to cast dramatically about: or is

anything I tear down mine to tear
down: or is everything torn-down

mine, burr & red spine of the lizard

flower: I am a lazy girl who won't learn
the names of the fruits:

what my father worked for to give me
I dream about giving away

running off into the spring night

mother, I walked to the bluest
lake / seeking it / mother / I wanted

the untrembling blue / that meant
I was good / wanting is sometimes

/ a small hole that opens in the
wall of the heart / that is how

my grandmother died / in Mumbai
/ which the Indians call Bombay

/ if you grow up with the colonizer's
/ words on the tongue they become

home / sometimes / wanting
is an open blossom / at the

wall of the heart / the
anonymous kind I plucked

from the schoolyard / where we pretended
the woods were home

handful of seed and whatever

spring you small-fevers age / you sweat-sheets
and long light / I am tired of the wrecked

world / here the day like awe-widened eyes /
here the blossoms insistent / the itch
in the eyelids insistent /

I don't mind the reeking of death /
don't mind the entrancing rich soil /
which is years of blazing-out bodies

I don't mind the wrinkles that
roost in the skin / or the draining of sun
from the organs / spring you small-fevers age

predawn, anthropocene

it is the color of streetlamps outside,
maddening bird-talk & porch-lights
on the red-brick public housing (again)
porches across the street, spring is still too
chilly for the street to be mine, pollen caught
in my hair, let my hair be the color
of a tangle of dirt. when I do not
know the neighbors after nearly
a year "because" they live in projects
—scatter the thrift-store bought glasses
from the table like angry cats, sink
& bolt & predawn hassle, & let
the imagined body break. take
the real body, look hard
at where the neighbors live,
look at the neighbors & go outside

Hurricane Watch

The slink of shirred clouds,
                blue-twitching. It is not here yet.

The slink of radar:
                watching families.

Adam likes the screens
                open. I close them

but like them open
                too. Sand and her people

on the steps.

If this is all a life is, watching,

childless, each person childless
                of her own certainty—

each person barren of
            certainty. Each man too,

each neighbor: so that
            when you look across

the street the neighbors
            are your own doubt.

No. No.

You are a spine of yellow
                tooth-rose in the rain,

spine of yellow
                flower, sea-spine,

brain that stars open, shines open,

forth-flower: I say this

to myself and to

Demetrius. He's with a friend

on bicycles, one wheel that matches
            his forest-green mountain bike

            and one pink-and-white
wheel from a girls' bike. He's in our carport

pumping at the wheel. Demetrius.

One month I called Shruti and said
            Demetrius is always here.

He pets the sweet cat Leela, the large
            silk-silver and ink-heat one. Demetrius

craning his head to Leela: *I want*

a cat like Leela. Demetrius at the door
      wants Adam.

I call Shruti: Demetrius always
            wants Adam.

What do we do? What do we do?

I will not call myself white
        but white guilt, white guilt

plasters my face as the storm

stirs in its pit. My in-laws

live in Florida, says Reg,
and they won't

leave. But it's time to
leave Florida. The South

of Florida is sinking.... and the storms

are three times as large,
says Reg. The storms are growing.

On Herman Street Demetrius
and his friends are

inside. The street is black-shine

and the trees green-whistle. Adam

is at work because he provides

an essential
service. Late morning, I'm alone

on Herman Street.

The storms are growing
and quick-silk vapor

on Herman Street flicks
along the alleys

where Lou's cat cases
the street, the kittens & mothers

     long carted away
in Adam's county truck to the shelter.

*

I can still do more
     than I have done

I realize in my thirties
     once the Lexapro

has taken root
in my blood, blood-root
trickster, insinuated
into my bloodstream
so that it is

necessary: so that despair follows

in its absence:

& did I invent
my own despair

from sheer wanting to say

like you I
have suffered. It turns out

that in late summer
of the end times

the air cools early,

brings its balm
to the sweat-soaked
fear of summer
early. In the yard

the moon starts to
double. I can't

tell: by the time
I look away

I can't tell
what I've invented.

Bildungsroman

I loved to get drunk. Drunkenness was a way

an identification—an eros

an absurdity, a blue-black longing.

like hours in a room with oneself.

to self-disgust—inside anyone's abjection.

"regardless of how wrecked, how stultifying"

"nowhere else to go."

Or—I don't want to be forgiven. Let the hard night

calling it "brown beer amber." I spoke her poem

I turned hard inside. I turned a hard star

I don't want to say, Vivian, the cold which is spoken

I don't want to say. Viv I the pale girl to your dark one

means something. Hard star at star's heart and the other

"The Unbearable Lightness of Being" in the skin folds

the idea of drug. It was drug of the spirit I wanted.

I am not mud / like the time after midnight

lets in pure moonlight / how moonlight

which is made of brittle names

how I put on a face / how I brought my face nearer

its mouth would blink to me

and veer nowhere. Make me a home then, silt one,

silk one, silk-dark-enough one, make me

Untitled (New Year's Eve & a Death Tucked Inside)

Who wants to go back? I was twenty-five that midnight in the yard of straight people with money, with a steampunk shack of odd objects and a sneaking old cat named Yvette at the doors' glass, black threaded with gray. Fear of cava: it rushes its cork at the night. This is how, I suppose, they undo their straightness and money, for all wholes want to dissolve. Edges mean desire to blur. This is why we get drunk, though I hope I won't again. But that night I was brave near the cava. Though I'd learned little of abandon from home. I come from straight people, all straightness is acting, for whom money was new-feathered and proud. So for me a clear edge to undo. So the hard-muscled and hard-eyed hurt beloved I'd found, who grew up in basements on welfare. Who loved to drink: I respected that love. So blazing cannons of cava cork shot at the night: the straight people liked our undoing dance and tried on their own. Theirs was good too. I am not ashamed to say I wasted some years then, one to three, on static misery punctuated by nights. It is sad but worlds are sadder. Cava, cava, then wine-dark—wine at parties can practice ongoing. But then hinges appear in the night, unseen doors between joy and the next thing. Three hours past midnight twenty-nine-year-old Esme was killed in her house. It was a man. I didn't know her but in my self-precious midnight tragedy's body I walked near her house as it happened. But not near enough to hear it until the next day's papers. Oh, I suddenly miss Austin, where this all happened—the kind of gentrifying city to which you can't go back: Wheatsville co-op with coconut water and a Buffalo Tofu Po'Boy, and the dream that the "man" is not you. I never felt Esme's pain but at Wheatsville I looked at a shrine to her. How I loved Wheatsville in my miserable youth among straight people—and *white* ones, I have forgotten to say; I have not even mentioned how white. That midnight, cava, cava, I feared no one loved my writing. It scared me when anyone loved anyone's writing. For who then was left to love mine? And it is hard to write so punctuated by nights. Except for the purest dark lyric, you can write that. But no one wants it. No one wants anything that pure—I am certain. I didn't but I couldn't tell. *Why don't you love me?* I screamed nightlong at Adam, the name of that beloved who is still, surprisingly, mine.

Summer Eighteen

My town stood alone
on a flat page of land.

My parents went to work.

A day was a big
maw-hole.

I tore some grass off
the edge of a yard.

Paced a junk aisle
of empty-bright wrappers.

I liked plastic chews
of sour sugar

and flame-heat-crunch
chemical spice.

My ex called to say
come suck me off.

I liked one drastic taste

to erase another,

leaving back-throat
wild jarring residues.

Later, I'd shit,
feeling half-cleaned

and okay.
Nights, I snapped

bored pictures
of my naked

mass. Pictures of
the mirror.

Sad nude with
black hairs.

In her hands
flashed a fascinating

crisis of light.

Hurricane Watch

Puerto Rico has no
                power. I text Jaquira

to say *I'm sorry,*
        how is your

family? Embarrassed because

I texted her so recently
—at the last blue-loosening

over the colonized
islands. Obvious mockery

        of us at the cost of
their houses. She doesn't

        text back. Screens shining

in my face, shining

and shining. To Adam
        home from work

I say a half-sentence

from deep in the news. But
                my dreams are all

about prettier girls

than me

& the books they've
        written. Oh, help—

I mutter one day
        into the picking-up
wind, but I forget
to ask it to slow. One night

the moon flickers off.
        It's like a screen

I've stared into
too long.

No.

I can do better.

*

Lexapro or belief in it
        has staunched

what it staunches. The womb
stays put, though
        empty. Now

I am laughing
in my house, overgrown,

long-legged, resigned

for now
to what I am. Some ragged pinks

are undone from their tight
knots before

my window. Laughing
        in my house

at the South of a continent
        in the ending-world.

*

Or I just mean
        resigned enough
to *live*. Depressives
of the present
        —long worn through

the case they built
        for their lives
—they get another
        chance.

False Quake

The sunburnt earth sudden.
          The people with their groceries

look up. The sunburnt
earth is a star

for an instant. Their phones
all shining. Their work

shining in the jilt
of their phones. Some not-sun

          faltered open.

For an instant the phones
blink off.

False Quake

Late September.

> Adam asks:
> have you noticed
> you haven't seen
> Lou in a while?

> She's bipolar.

How do you know?
(Jealously) did she tell you?

> Sand told me.

> Sand says when she gets in the pit she
> just stays in bed for days with the shades pulled.

Our house faces the projects,
faces Sand's house and Lou's
house. They are identical brick
but with flowers.

> This I have not seen
> in the other places I've lived
> before I moved here for the end
> times: flowers. The fiercest flowers
> they grow in the public
> housing. The huge
> face of a hibiscus plant
> stares me down with its stamen....

At this moment,
I am writing,
and Sand

is taking our tomatoes!
She has come over to
our tomato plant with shears
—an arrangement Adam
worked out.

But I went to pick tomatoes
yesterday: they were bad.

I cut one open: they have
a terrible lunge of green
inside them.

I bought organic tomatoes
from the market instead!

      And now I look up
      and Lou is here.

      To take more tomatoes.

      —in a sundress
      with sunglasses.

      And smiling.

      Over fifty
      and lean—Lou & Mitch
      are the only
      white people
      on their side of the street.

Mitch gruff & working
on motorcycles.

I try to drive to pick up Amy

to take her to the church

where we tutor teens on DACA.

But it is the day I didn't count my Lexapro
& took two. & so I drive
over a curb. & so

two tires pop, heat-pop,
the southern small city
crawling home from work. The rims
are scraping the ground.
& so many drive by.
Do you need help? Need help?

Amy comes and laughs
at the tires.

Then she walks on
to tutor the teens alone.

First she takes a picture of me
        frowning beside
my car so the teens
        will believe me.

So many white boys
pull up behind my car—

placed so that two lanes
of rush-hour traffic
have to merge into one.

The tow-truck man comes.

        I am wearing office
clothes, looking ready

        to show these teens
I can help.

                He says:
                I'll give you a ride.

        No, I can walk:

the dusk has cooled
and I'm ready to walk.

                That's not a safe
                neighborhood, where you live.

                College students
                live there too.

                These college students,
                living in the hood!

                No wonder they get robbed.

No wonder they get
beaten up....

I say nothing.

My brain smudged
with twice as much Lexapro
as it's supposed to contain

or maybe just full of
a normal day....

Sara Ahmed says
that we are taught to fear
the *stranger.* I live among
strangers.

His name is Michael,
the driver—he wants my

approval. It is like the time
four years ago
when I was arrested for drunk
driving and they said:

you don't look like someone
who should be in jail.
        And I said: *nothing.*
Because I was fingerprinted
        and *in jail.*

They don't bring up
these kids
the right way anymore,

Michael says.

They don't hit
them.

I would never
get a DUI,

Michael says. If I'd got

one, I'dve told them
keep me in here
fifty years.

And here I said:
nothing.

But this is the thing:
across the street,

at Lou's house,
Michael *waves* to
Mitch.

You know Mitch?

Yeah! I say.

Here in the "hood,"
Michael waves to Mitch.

Mitch is white,
remember.

*

Not fall,
but a flare of winter

in summer's
heart. How a wild sudden

snow, how ice flickers
awake in the air

of the green South

& how snow

is a sharper asking.

Their statues
of the old

men who gritted
their teeth

and were proud

are on the
streets. Sand

has more people
staying

at her house.

*

I did not earn

I did not earn

no one earns

storm-drain, storm-wasted
storm-thick other

not other earned more
than other steeped quick
seafoam other
seabrittle other
who waits in the drunk year

sea-altered other
dusk-rose
drink-rose

These are the names we say in the storm

These are the teeth that grit
at the storm. Did you fill
the bathtub? Did you drench
the storm quick?

How storm can grow
from a year. How storm

can grow quick-brittle,
dusk-brittle. I asked

the women to come
to my house. The cowrie

shells rose, tooth-
gritted rose, stuck
in concrete: stuck so
hard and good. Stuck
gritted. Stuck
gritted, a person

in a storm. Stuck gritted
—the tall spines
of green plastic
to hang the tomatoes
—gone stronger
than frail nature. The smog
that turns the sunsets
flare-orange.

The hurricane
comes. The one teacher thought
she could not teach, thought
everyone better. The neighbors
are inside. The purple

all dusk-caught in her nail polish.
The pink gold of her
ring, the steeple-teeth
in a ring. What if

she was not good
at anything? Taught
falter or star-teeth
they made the others
sing. They were captured-
tooth and they were
brittle-face. I could not
stop the rage
or rustling, could
not better the
tapped-night blunt-
out. Could not.

She is throwing her
black paint at the sheets
scattered on her sun-flicked
floor. Painter desperate
to make something
of herself. But it is not
just one person one should
save. Still she wants
to make herself great
before the world ends.

Stuck, end-stuck

Stuck, end-stuck

Stuck, end-stuck

The neighbors are inside.

Adam is at work,
providing an essential service.

There are no more neighbors
in the green South, which I could pretend
is my own house. There are no more
neighbors here.

Sand is not on her porch:
            two hours ago, wing-tethered

and sand-stuck. Once Sand

was leaving our house and I saw
a cobweb quick over her twists

            sweet wind in the cobwebs.

Red-peach. Red-peach

—I should have beaten
it away with a broom

Later Adam follows
            me to bed. There

is red-peach caught

in me, lodged there.
He teases it out

            —I squirm while

his thick fingers work.

No more, no other
red-stepped licking

in the end times. No more

sand, no more Sand

*

I think to call everyone
I have known. *Is it*

ending faster
over there? The river

the river; I speak
into hands; river

They ask the river
all throttled, all sun
all sun all rain all
the night is quick

They stare into
the screens all
quick-flicking,
silver-nib. No.

Teacher. Seed.
Seed. On our tarot
cards the pictures of the
disappeared cities.

There is a heat
near the heat-

plant when I move
my hand. Fault-year

is a quick
teacher. Fault-
year is a tall
seed-struggle. Fault-
year, not fast, not
broken, not
other-faced, fault-year.

No.

In a Cathedral of Only Dark

Rothko Chapel, Houston, early new year

In every black there is
violet. I am speaking to you,

violet. When you come to the
precipice of your life and sit
in the dark.

Once a woman
drove out where
        the stars sharpened

hard. I am writing this
on the back
of a receipt. The stars sharpen

like there's desperate light
behind. I like ugly dialect
best. And roots

that rattle in the frozen
soil. Black alive wires
wanting out of

themselves. I
quit drinking
so that I would find

this, the world
a frail hull. How a coin

of false gold twinkles

on the floor
of an empty
room. I took drink away

knowing it meant I would trudge
a black sand beach
past trash-strewn harbor towns

a long time. Knowing
I would trudge. But how long

is the dark? A man blackens
a canvas
alone. Tired child, you are lost

a long time. How the old years of joy
lodge in you like fevered
stars. Worn-wood lodge

in some forest, the present.
I am saying there is good

in asking, good in asking again,
good in staring and asking. Though I don't

know. How the dark is made
of so many

smudges, how you can call
that prayer.

How dark is made
of bareness, of

doors, of gold.

Tritina for Joseles, for Mirrors, for Those
I Won't Know, for Ashes & Rising

Once I tried to write a book about a mirror,
but I got too distracted by the dirt
that clung to my own body. I named dirt "failure"

then. I was terrified of failure
then, though it was all I knew: my mirror.
This week I don't care: I learned too much from dirt

this week, Joseles in the dirt, the dirt
on other men's faces. The police know failure
but don't understand yet. We are all so scared of mirrors,

but this is a mirror in dirt, and I refuse more failure.

In memoriam Joseles De La Cruz Ornelas, 1984–2016

Structure Crossing Danger

Coffee spilled on a stone. Xenon, stranger.
When lax my mind excites. It is a strange
mind, mine. But the strangeness not mine. Mind
is strange. Anaxagoras' line. Experience
turns mind to xenon. Not mine alone, strangeness. Not mine,
mind. I spilled coffee on the stone of a search.
A church. I can't drink coffee. Anaxagoras? I love nothing
more than coffee: except mind. And wine. Late coffee.
Mind is closer to wine than I knew. Spilled coffee
on the stone of a church and wondered
madly if it would stain. X, stranger. There is a boredom
in madness, I learned inside it. Some of us long and long
for madness till we're there. It is sweet
to come close, mad one. X. There is madness
in whiteness. In madness
white silence from the page blares. When mad
the mind excites. Mine does. Turns laxness
to madness. If you have not been to madness
don't go. Come close enough to look.
I love nothing more than my mind
except my body. And nothing more than my body
except my mind. And nothing more
than either except the world. And nothing
more than the world except
for rain. And nothing more than rain except mind.
And nothing more than mind besides wine.
No one loves madness. Here
is coffee spilled on a stone.

Marquee

News of the end in the air
is a hot-mouth blossom. Faltered blossom.
Then the newspapers one day
come out blank. Adam teases
the blue plastic
from the doorstep paper:
sweet grey, empty. The birds jabber
in the wakened sun.
I have nicked
the old maroon Honda
more. Each day we live
I accidentally some more
strip its dark paint from
the dull-eyed metal. It waits in the drive
where they laid
the pale paper.
Deme across the street
turns twelve
in a t-shirt of tulip-orange. The boys
are on bikes, looping
the streets. It is light until nine
through January. Wrong season.
Like the blue taste of terrible
gin. I would like to be a boy
this freak summer.

Evening mouthy
in her blue dress.

Marquee

The news has been in the air
                    for months. News of the end.

WHAT DO YOU WANT
                    BEFORE IT IS OVER?

The companies are selling
                    furiously. Bright signs

in the windows. I have never
                    seen my neighbors

downtown.

Marquee: HAVE A COLD DRINK
BEFORE THE WORLD ENDS.

The cold stayed for two weeks. I hate
the cold: frozen sweater pulled to

my neck. Then it melted. Then

the blossoms came early: mouth-flower in violet

to the bare-branched bush. In January

the year new-fingered with pearl-flower

too early. One morning I went

to campus early and saw Demetrius

waiting for the school bus, staring

alone at a scarlet knot of rose.

A PhD student is smoking on my neighbor's

porch. *I think this is a capitalist*

invention. The stores in the center of town

are bedecked with HURRY. *I'll believe*

it when things are free.

Before I quit drinking

this student and I went to the bars

in the largeness of spring

evening. He spoke seriously

about the end times. He wore

black glasses. I felt indignant:

You believe that?

But you are doing

nothing.

He was never

at the protests.

Now he has reversed

his belief.

I would like

to ask the others.

The rest of us

are furious, green-furious.

Fury of green

and orange. I call my mother

on the West Coast, where

it has gone dry. I call her

each Sunday.

I don't believe

it, she says.

There are no flowers

there. She comes to visit

and gasps. Blossom.

And:

I forgot

about green.

How They Speak of the Fields

For us. They say:

just dig your hands

into the good, good

soil of the field

and you will grow into a child

of our heart. Be quiet

and work, for you are good

at it, for you are almost

a child of our heart

already. Listen

and we will reward

you. We will reward

you, but don't talk

—you will want to

have earned the

reward. We will

reward you later, much,

much later. Are you not

a child of the field, a child

native to the field?

But I have never seen

the field. I was born

in it but squeezed

my eyes shut. I squeezed

my eyes hard shut

so I could imagine

another field....

Want at Least Evening

I am scared to write,
                    but tired of speaking

of failure. It's summer.
                    I am ashamed because I love

the heat. Wet hair and all
                    grasses yielding to anything.

 Sit on the step while the wet
                    deepens on the edge of drink. Long

craving for undoing. To sit alone
                    and watch the day in its lapse of thought.

When you grow up want turns
                    specific: thirst or victual, rough

gentle hand on the back. I taught myself my
                    vices. Wine with a flicker of citrus,

evening, anything
                    that goes on and on. Anyone

who would hold me in his gaze
                    and forgive.

I spent a few years on the city's
                    slumping side because I wanted

to know: is all desperation
                    the same? I used to wander

the yard calling for a sleek
               creature made of moon on the

branches. Waiting for his
               silk purr on my legs and shaking

a handful of keys. Is all
               desperation the same?

I can't tell, eyeholes flushed
               fresh. I am scared. I would

like to abscond
               from the category called

woman. There is in it
               too much pacing

a desolate garden
               peeling bark from the

trees. Trying to transfix
               with a smile. Mother

at my age
               in some kitchen

married but want-wild
               no matter. Whichever

cup fills with what you
               can bear. In this town

night lingers farther
                    away. But make your

list of humble
                    tasks. Move to the

margin of daytime.
                    Discard whatever

breaks. I wish I could understand
                    suffering as something

shared. I speak in a kind
                    voice to a man at the

laundromat: he stinking
                    and changing his pants

by the long wall of
                    dryers. Feet swelling

in slippers.
                    I pour him a little

detergent. I speak in a kind
                    voice but not without

fear. Now the day won't turn off,
                    long slumping day of my

sadness. I want at least
                    evening to wear itself

cooler. Day won't wear
                    down. I find myself with

nothing to ask. How to make
                    nothing of what you

spoke once. I can't find you
                    and June has passed down

its favors to never. I've done
                    my chores. I'm done

with aching for today
                    but not heartbroken

yet. Just tired of watching
                    for lateness, tired of

watching a face
                    waiting for the love

to click off.
                    I know how the air feels

on both sides of desire
                    and on neither can you

place your palms on the table,
                    say *done.*

One Who Are We

One low night. A low night.

We are good at low nights

in our house of flail.

Our rain it steams from itself.

The stars they twined quick and untwined.

Lou's house: a flamingo-lily.

River-lily, star-lily. Sand's: porch women

in red dresses now and then

& their bodies made large hot

shapes. I wanted more from myself.

I wanted more.

But I asked Adam if we could make

a child. *Now,* I said. The stars

are hot questions but so distant

you forget. A word is a night-thrown

question. And so I pressed coconut

oil in me to clear his passage

inward. So this is the most reckless

making. Let it be. The earth

is dying. We have heat.

Final April

How it has run up on us with the seeds in its teeth

of blossoms. Demetrius asked me:

are you having a kid? I have turned visible

I have grown visible as someone

other than myself. I have grown to woman

Heavy woman with night-seed

of a kind man

In her belly. I am reading about *hyperobjects*

an idea we can't face

the end is too large for the size

of the mind. I know nothing beyond

the neighborhood. It is too

large-throated itself, the bird cries

in the world-throat. Since the heat

they have started to gather

for night and song. I leave open

the window. We cook

with the screen to their

night. *Come inside.*

I want to grow full

with you too.

Nightslip

Six a.m., April, the world opens its eyes in the dark.
A man on his verandah after a night of gin.
Bitter blue leached from him by hours.
Now just the shaky greeting of morning.
The dark on his side of the house only.
Then the dark on no sides.
His friend, hectic-eyed earlier,
on the floor asleep.

If there is no meaning to this
there are at least people in neighborhoods
who come to the edge of a porch.
There are trees with white blossom in their fists.

Maybe Another

Maybe there will be another

world. Maybe the insistent

birds, busy. Who is awake

in the neighborhoods now?

Six a.m., seven—

When it is over I will say only

that I loved this waking

—that I loved it most—

How I wake alone all

battered by my own wrongs but

awake there is someone else

There are wide

and wide-eyed watchers

Night is another eye

Night is a sweet eyelet

I want to belong

to this world. It is

a strange thing to say.

I want to belong.

Before it ends

I want the town hall

of the world

to do nothing but

gather.

I want us all to gather

in the foam of the night

that is sloughing away

as day starts. Maybe

a cafeteria of everyone

I want to belong.

I will gather with anyone

How it leaks away always.

I will gather still.

Midnight, Sober

(in the kitchen watching
the silk of dark
 wear itself
 transparent)

When I was nine
I once went wrongly
to a dance class

for children who
knew how to dance.

The teacher
pulled my mother
aside.

At that moment
I was leaping
and kicking,
believing myself

in subtle
accord.

Teacher moved
the delicate

swallowing muscles

in her pale
craned neck.

Grown now, to want
to articulate

is to love
to fail.

Landscape in the Sulk of June

June year. how the mouths of us grow large
       how the doves pecking in the slip of the night

how the night has not gone yet
       from the wakeful bed of the morning

& morning stretches. morning in its first flick
       morning the blue that peels from the year

May year. how the year is slipping away
       from itself. how time goes like this

though I would hold it
       though I would make

small work & hold—though the year
       goes careful—though

April year. April year
       there is no salt slipping this way

salt which makes ours. salt
       in the careful eyes

in the careful eyes of the March year
       my love & his prayer

my love and this one—how joy
       let it stay

Final Neon

Last night I ate neon seeds of sugar, late.

The bag from a worn station.

The gas pumps lurking

outside, large witness. Inside

waiting to see if the numbers

would blaze into a win.

I bought my Chewy Sweet Tarts

there, the bag purple

-battered, blue. $1.79. Outside

beneath the dark the blossoms

stayed wide-mouthed, like women

talking late. But I was alone.

City at the world's end:

time gone to soft dark.

The belly-child kicking.

Wanting out. Wanting out

for an instant with the blossoms.

Before the dark closes.

I drove home, twitching sweet-sick.

I won't eat that sugar

again. When the end is soon

you can surrender your vices.

I don't want a drink.

The Moment You Become Aware, You're Free

Through the rain shimmer
          the rest of the world: what's left.

I am meditating,
      using an app—and my shining

coral-pale phone was made
             from hard labor in mines.

The screen of rain here
        could be their faint hammering.

But now it's over.

How hard it was for the world to matter to me.

I wanted this pale body to be that:

not just me, but a door. I want it still.

I want the world in my body. The imploding night.

The curls of the tongue of stars. I'm selfish;

the door out of me creaks

like the creak in the bones of everyone

I never thought about as they

stood in the death instant. Trick world.

Last night I opened the windows

to screens and labored for hours

over an enchilada that tasted okay.

Song & Procrastination Song

Then an April winter
                    over the town

like one cold marble. The neighbors

withdraw. Cold marble

alone in my hands.   At the doctor's

they measure my child

        as if we are

all statues. As if we'll

persist. The world

        a cold brimming drink. Not

yet spilled. Still the flowers

        large as a face. In a warehouse

back of town   there are meetings

to provide free services

when the end comes.   Everyone

in the meetings (but me) is white, ragged-clothes

        grad students. And earnest

church faces.   White—how it wanted

to get out of itself—to rattle

        free of its trap.   Around

them, the good whites

        I turn white too:

so white this wanting

                to be clean.   History

is nearer at the end. The end

        is the face of history

with its boils and blood.   I wrap

myself against the cold and go out.

House & House & Town & End

Yesterday Genevieve came over
        to read tarot. My cards are black,

witchy, black—spare rays of white
      etched on them.   I want to learn

my mother's gods.   At the end of the world surrounded

by gods.   We hold our dark cards close.

The gods turn their faces
        from me.   I know

they are there—
           The town is holding
              its mayoral election,

a black man—in these politics a long time

running against a white progressive—at the library

       today. I am going.

I will go first to the meeting   about the world's

ending. Every
      meeting: ending, ending.

Who can we   protect?

       If the world lasts until

                    I become mother

will I turn away   from their faces
        turn in over   my small one
—or could I be
                    to the world

force of silk and dark: mother

force of green rain

before it ends: silk, firefly, warm palms
                       to a fire. Sheltering dark cat.
                       Page of names. Page & its dark
                       of prayer. Friend.

Despair as Stars Long Ago Blinked Out

The town is so small—I have walked its
                          green streets, among its blossoms

looking for someone
                    to talk to—looking

to be among friends. (But what
                            does it mean, house, road,

a lizard hot green with a red throat?) And also

it is larger than I know.
                    100,000 people—imagine

all their thoughts smudging
                    this page. Imagine their minds

coming so close—imagine the thoughts

all inking—the page would be so crowded.

Right now I am alone at my desk.

Fear Is a Rose of Hot Pink and Gold

The trouble is

that fear is a rose you carry alone.

       Carry it through the steam-green
streets.   Carry it in front

of your face

like a cross of sweets

like a wished-for despair

No, I don't want
         the rubble when

the world ends—no

I don't want to watch

Demetrius die

       a stranger   and I am too
                scared
to say to him:
          be my child.

The streets of the town
         are ordinary

though quiet. They are not printing

news of the end, because

no one knows.
                    No one knows

what news means.

        One day a crescent sliver

        caught in an orange-fire

        sky.   This week

        the Internet

                            went cold
again.
Instead of screens

        one another's eyes.

(No One is the name of a fear.

        No One as a silk ribbon caught
            in an ear.)

                    Adam goes to work
                                still—

I have grown a lump on my leg

        that is a fluid pooled
        beneath the skin in a careful

clutch. What fluid. What speaking. It is not
speaking—

Midwife 1: probably just something weird in your veins

Midwife 2: Let's ask a surgeon

Surgeon's nurse: how strange

Surgeon: I don't know
let's check in three months

Though in three months—what? In three months what

will be left. Don't ask too

much. The night

stay grown. Who knows if the world

will be

in three months

star of a world. World like cinnamon candy

on the tongue now and then later

gone.   Jasper is kicking

inside me—world, let me see

you a night mint.

you a mint from hotel in a palm

you a sucked sweet mint—we went to the store

Adam & I when we
              spoke again—he can barely

come into the house without
              my yelling in

his ear: no

no is a deer brought forth

out of the long green that twists

this way then again

snakes like a first

black squiggle—Amy & I saw it

on the path.   She said: *I like snakes*
                              they mean something
                                      to me.

What?

              a change

Chicopee-Dudley is the name

of this neighborhood in Athens, Georgia.

The Confederate Armory was here.

There was a child here who wanted

to buy a baby basket for her doll—

she was willing to pay $15—I learned

this before the Internet went.

Sirens are the sound of jeweled red.

They built a new path here.

A siren is distant

until it comes for your home. A siren is

a throttle / I will speak my mouth

to its ear, a green

that is a salt. I wanted to remember

I want to remember

though how to remember

when *we* are gone.   Reg says:

there will *be* the earth,
and it will wait,

a being with dirt
            in its mouth—spoon of a being

it will wait

I am always failing

myself. I was built

the failing bank of a river, blue thwart

blue chortle—I worry

a hangnail—it goes failed-blue

and quick.

If I fail myself every day until the world ends. The turtles flip in the
stream still. I don't want to see them die. Can I fail outward—can I
fail the boundaries of my own skin so that I am released into the
neighborhood. So that I am near the turtle—my skin and its the hurt
purple that takes the stars inside itself. In the long moon shadow
we turn hurt purple that way. Can I peel my skin to its core and
otherwise turn it—can I peel the core to hot gold. Can I go more
than no night that is a person. Jasper in an envelope at the end of
a womb.

Landscape After Years With Yourself (World's End)

here all want is for itself,
        bare spine of the heat day,

        want is upright
when everything else

wilts.
        I wanted

        what was exact and true,
bare spine

of the heat day,
        for want itself I gave up

        everything,
bare spine of the heat day

bent cross
        in the heat. wilted cross

        I came to the bare spine to save us
all want is for itself.

wilted cross,
        all want is for itself.

        cross wilted on the spine of the heat day
spine of the heat day

        want is
hard and sticks beneath the skin of feelings

even if someone is lost here
      the flat heat speaks to no one

      all want is for itself
wilting cross, the heat keeps on

Noise Is the Daughter of Morning

There are trails all over
                    the neighborhood, trails

the city made: once

they made them for us. And now

they will be left

at the end. Kristen and I

walk over to the park

and boys are playing soccer, brown-skinned

boys are playing. *Let us play.*

They are ten-year-old boys
            and we are two pale

giants, eyes full

with end.   How I wanted so much

to be brown, how I wanted it

in this world until it ended. Wanted

for my mother a river

where the brown-skinned bathe—brown chant
            of voices. The kindness

in the eyes large.   And I will go

as a pale tower with the brown in me
                    pulsing. I will go along the edge

of the field, which is a river. Pale crystal
                    of a body—

I will offer you to the river

of voices.   *Can we play*

says Kristen.   At her voice someone turns

—Demetrius.   *Hey!* he yells, surprised.

        (it's Adam's wife

the white girl from his street)—Once

a girl asked me: *do you go to our school?*

a girl and her friend on bikes   —hot pink beads

in their hair—*They have big*

kids there.   I was thirty then

and now I am older.
                    But no one

is any age when   the world ends—

not in the moment
        of ending—it will   end here

a field a river, and daffodils
                    raise their hot throats—

Kristen is among the boys
                        & I watch her

turn boy, soccer ball   like a rare

dappled seed,   and the noon

is whole in the knowing of ending. The boys
                    deserved a better world.

Across the city   the garden holds
        song to us, song to face

& eye.   Deme is next to me
            watching Kristen—large & white-blonde of skin

still but the boys rushing her
                & Deme turned like me watching.

Final April

By the Confederate
        Armory at the world's

end. I've walked past it for years.

Now the months
            don't have names.

Now I've become small.

No I've always been small.

It is made of brick.
        Brick is hard

to burn—but in the neighborhood

we've decided to burn it.

        We walk past a stretch
of black road pulled up

        cast up a night of road
how road made a name
            of a steeple, road

made a sound that was home.

We come with our
            buckets of fire

Deme, then Sand—Lou and Mitch

—someone said

but my great- grandfather
          worked there. He was

a good man.

          Sand said:

          I agree he was good.
                    The good
          were caught in this too.

I want Jasper to be born
          the night of this

burning. My mother brought
          her tiny gods of old silver

to me on my wedding
          and I bring them now
  to watch.

Ganesha and Saraswati.
          Shiva.

The ones who work
          in this building

are ready to stop. In their
          office clothes they file

out. There are four brown
                    women among them.

I want to say: *say I am one of you.*

When the world ends say I am here.

Porch Summer in the Past

Nine years ago I met Adam:
                    on a porch in East Austin

—it was a hot green place
                    on the world's edge

I thought. I walked the neighborhood
                    then, it was like

this one: families and elders

eyeing white gentrifiers.

Eyeing, watering can in hand. I spindly, pale,
                    but tanned as brown as I could—

and we sat on the porch then
                    and drank. And drank. And then

a green hot undoing could unreel

in a person, and we revered it.
                    We revered

undoing.... how history

tugged in a person. Now I am growing
                    his child. To bear

a child is to come to the death mouth.

With the body a cup of all
               the elixir we wanted

to drink. To hold the body as a quiet
                    offering and say

I want the world. I want it to stay.

Henry Dumas, author of this book's epigraph, was killed at 33 by a policeman. He was active in the Black Power and Civil Rights movements. Toni Morrison calls him "an absolute genius."

"Bildungsroman" quotes from Hilton Als' essay "It Will Soon Be Here" in *White Girls*.

Poems from this book appeared first in these journals: *7 × 7 LA*, *Anomaly*, *Bennington Review*, *Copper Nickel*, *Eleven Eleven*, *Gulf Coast*, *Nat. Brut*, *Poetry*, *Poetry Northwest*, *TAYO Literary Journal*, *The Elephants*, *The Missouri Review*, *Timber*, and *Waxwing*.

They were reprinted in *Bettering American Poetry Vol. 2*, *Poetry Daily*, *Vandal*, and *Verse Daily*.

Thank you to all the editors for their work on behalf of poetry, and for publishing mine.

Thank you to Zach for publishing the book and to Jon for designing it.

Thank you to my teachers, especially Brigit Pegeen Kelly and Andrew Zawacki, and also Reg McKnight, Tricia Lootens, and Ed Pavlić. Thank you to my friends, especially Shruti Swamy, who is tireless in her belief. Thank you to Shruti, Emma Catherine Perry, and Lindsay Tigue for reading drafts, and for your own work. Thank you to Alexandra Mattraw for museship. Thank you to Carolina Ebeid, Leanna Petronella, and Kevin Powers: four forever. Thank you to Kristen Gleason, Gabrielle Lucille Fuentes, and Amy Bonnaffons. Thank you to Ben Rutherfurd, Gina Abelkop, Jacob Sunderlin, Ginger Ko, and Genevieve Arlie for your readings and thoughts. Thank you to Kundiman, which changed my poetic life, and to Sarah Gambito especially. Thank you to Adam for pressing me to finish my Kundiman application when my mettle almost failed me.

Thank you to every neighbor and stranger I attempted to represent in this book. I take responsibility for anything I got wrong.

Thank you to Adam and Jasper—and Vijaya, Timothy, and Patrick—for giving me a home in the world, burning or no.

Late Morning When the World Burns
was printed in an edition of 250 copies
on Glatfelter 55# Natural Offset Antique
by McNaughton & Gunn

Text was set in Artigo and Monument Grostesk

Design by Jon Grizzle